PLEASE

New Issues Poetry & Prose

Editor   William Olsen

Managing Editor   Marianne Swierenga

Copy Editor   Natalie Giarratano

Assistant Editors   Adam Clay & Kimberly Kolbe

New Issues Poetry & Prose
The College of Arts and Sciences
Western Michigan University
Kalamazoo, MI 49008

Sixth Printing, 2015.

ISBN-10   1-930974-79-5 (paperbound)
ISBN-13   978-1-930974-79-1 (paperbound)

Library of Congress Cataloging-in-Publication Data:
Brown, Jericho
Please/Jericho Brown
Library of Congress Control Number: 2008923669

Art Director   Tricia Hennessy
Designer   Adrianne Mesnard
Production Manager   Paul Sizer
                      The Design Center, Frostic School of Art
                      College of Fine Arts
                      Western Michigan University
Printing   McNaughton & Gunn, Inc.

PLEASE

JERICHO BROWN

New Issues

WESTERN MICHIGAN UNIVERSITY

Contents

POWER

STOP

Acknowledgements:

Earlier versions of these poems appeared in the following journals and anthologies:

AGNI Online: "Rick"
American Literary Review: "Idea for an Album: *Vandross, the Duets*"
Barrow Street: "Family Portrait"
Bloom: "I Have Just Picked up a Man"
Born Magazine: "Prayer of the Backhanded" (reprint)
Broadsided Press: "Open" (reprint)
Callaloo: "Grip," "Like Father," "Open," "Scarecrow"
Drumvoices Revue: "Detailing the Nape"
Hayden's Ferry Review: "Track 3: (Back down) Memory Lane"
Indiana Review: "Lion," "Beneath Me" (published as "All That Crawls beneath Me")
The Iowa Review: "Track 5: Summertime"
jubilat: "Robert," "Tin Man"
New England Review: "Because My Name Is Jericho," "Prayer of the Backhanded"
Pleiades: "The Gulf"
Poetry International: "David"
Post Road: "Track 1: Lush Life," "Track 4: Reflections"
Prairie Schooner: "The Burning Bush," "Herman Finley Is Dead," "Pause"
Water–Stone Review: "Again"

"Detailing the Nape" appeared in *Gathering Ground: A Cave Canem 10-year Anniversary Anthology*, The University of Michigan Press.

"Beneath Me" (published as "All That Crawls Beneath Me") appeared in a chapbook of poems *Indiana Review* developed for promotional purposes at the 2008 AWP Conference.

"Because My Name Is Jericho" appeared in *The Poetry of Recovery*, Sante Lucia Books.

"Like Father" appeared in *The Ringing Ear*, University of Georgia Press.

"Detailing the Nape" and "Lunch" (published as "Sign Language for the Mute") appeared in *Role Call: A Generational Anthology of Social and Political Black Literature and Art*, Third World Press.

"Like Father" and "Prayer of the Backhanded" appeared in *The Weight of Addition: An Anthology of Texas Poetry*, Mutabilis Press.

"My Parents Snoring" appeared in *Working Hard for the Money: America's Working Poor in Stories, Poems, and Photos*, Bottom Dog Press.

Several of these poems were written with support from the Bread Loaf Writer's Conference, the Callaloo Creative Writing Workshops, the Cave Canem Workshop/Retreat, the City of New Orleans Mayor's Office of Communications (1998-2002), Dillard University, *Gulf Coast: A Journal of Literature and Fine Arts*, Houston Community College-Southeast Campus, the Krakow Poetry Seminar in Poland, the NOMMO Literary Society, PoZazz Productions, the University of Houston Creative Writing Program and Inprint, Inc., the University of New Orleans Creative Writing Department, the University of San Diego, and the University of Texas Medical Branch Youth Environmental Studies Laboratory School.

Gratitude also goes to the following teachers and friends for commenting on this book or its poems at various stages of development: Rick Barot, Randy Bates, Remica Bingham, Brian Blanchfield, Tameka L. Cage, Kyle Dargan, Nequella Demery, Amber Dermont, Mark Doty, Michael Dumanis, Katie Farris, Nikky Finney, Nick Flynn, Ross Gay, Gloria Wade Gayles, John Gery, Jennifer Grotz, Kimiko Hahn, James Hall, Forrest Hamer, Terrance Hayes, Sean Hill, Tony Hoagland, Major Jackson, Tyehimba Jess, Amaud Johnson, Ilya Kaminsky, Douglas Kearney, Yusef Komunyakaa, Andrew Kozma, Loren Kwan, Mark McKee, Jane Miller, Kay Murphy, Antonya Nelson, Steve Orlen, Monica Parle, Chivas Perkins, Bob Phillips, Claudia Rankine, Roger Reeves, Kalamu ya Salaam, Mona Lisa Saloy, Charlton Seward, Richard Siken, Tracy K. Smith, Charles Springfield, Natasha Trethewey, Addie Tsai, David Ray Vance, Ellen Bryant Voigt, John Weir, Susan Wood, Tiphanie Yanique, and Patricia Yongue.

"The beautiful ones always smash the picture."
—Prince Rogers Nelson

REPEAT

Track 1: Lush Life

The woman with the microphone sings to hurt you,
To see you shake your head. The mic may as well
Be a leather belt. You drive to the center of town
To be whipped by a woman's voice. You can't tell
The difference between a leather belt and a lover's
Tongue. A lover's tongue might call you *bitch*,
A term of endearment where you come from, a kind
Of compliment preceded by the word *sing*
In certain nightclubs. A lush little tongue
You have: you can yell, *Sing bitch*, and, *I love you*,
With a shot of Patrón at the end of each phrase
From the same barstool every Saturday night, but you can't
Remember your father's leather belt without shaking
Your head. That's what satisfies her, the woman
With the microphone. She does not mean to entertain
You, and neither do I. Speak to me in a lover's tongue—
Call me your bitch, and I'll sing the whole night long.

Prayer of the Backhanded

Not the palm, not the pear tree
Switch, not the broomstick,
Nor the closest extension
Cord, not his braided belt, but God,
Bless the back of my daddy's hand
Which, holding nothing tightly
Against me and not wrapped
In leather, eliminated the air
Between itself and my cheek.
Make full this dimpled cheek
Unworthy of its unfisted print
And forgive my forgetting
The love of a hand
Hungry for reflex, a hand that took
No thought of its target
Like hail from a blind sky,
Involuntary, fast, but brutal
In its bruising. Father, I bear the bridge
Of what might have been
A broken nose. I lift to you
What was a busted lip. Bless
The boy who believes
His best beatings lack
Intention, the mark of the beast.
Bring back to life the son
Who glories in the sin
Of immediacy, calling it love.
God, save the man whose arm
Like an angel's invisible wing
May fly backward in fury
Whether or not his son stands near.
Help me hold in place my blazing jaw
As I think to say, *excuse me.*

Track 3: (Back down) Memory Lane

Dangerous men park carefully,
Slanting over-sized automobiles
Into the ditches that line
77th. It's Friday night
In Shreveport. Checks
Have been cashed, bills
Folded and stashed
Into wallets and bra straps.
Card tables, folding chairs,
And every gold-tooth in town
Crowd our grandmother's
Camelback shotgun house
Because gambling's illegal
In Shreveport and she cuts
Only two dollars a hand
For every joker that slides
Into a queen. We don't know
Minnie Riperton's dead
Years now, buried
With one breast to her name.
School-uniformed in a corner,
We learn to listen to music
Over hollers, through
Smoke. Her soprano comes across
A photograph in giggles,
But ends up crying,
Save me. We think we'd like that
Kind of love, sad and steeped
In trumpets, though a block up
The entire decade shoots
For words to put in the dictionary:
Crackhead, drive-by. Loss

9

And gain. The bullet
Meant for a man named Money
Removes his baby sister's chin.
Ask for horns in Shreveport
And sirens are on the way.
We can't hear either, grandmama
Calling for us to change
The tape, *No more slow songs,*
Keep us awake, these years
Before surgeons slice her
In vain, and we drive
Away, our car stereos
Playing rhythm and blues.

Track 4: Reflections

—as performed by Diana Ross

I wanted to reflect the sun.

I wore what glitters, smiled,
Left my eyes open, and

On the ceiling of my mouth,

Balanced a note as long as God allowed,
My head tilted backwards, my arms stretched

Out and up, I kept praying,

If the red sun rising makes a sound,
Let my voice be that sound.

I could hear the sun sing in 1968.

I learned the word *assassin*
And watched cities burn.

Got another #1 and somebody

Set Detroit on fire. That was power—
White folks looking at me

Directly and going blind

So they wouldn't have to see
What in the world was burning black.

Scarecrow

*"In a field
I am the absence
of field."*
—Mark Strand

I. To Dorothy

Everyone needs something to hang onto.
It helps us keep the crows away.

You cling to your journey—
A long walk on yellow brick, two taps

From a wizard's wand. I like to think
Of these cornrows as a kind of maze,

Imagine unhitching myself
From this pole I'll never call home

And walking through stalks to an end
Where, like magic, someone touches me.

II. At Picnic

If you stand where I hang
And keep your eyes straight,
You will see a poplar
At the far edge of the field. There,
A body once swayed,
Burning from foot to breast.
The crows cawed
Unmoved, their plucking a parade.
The wind blew the odor of death

In my direction. I had a mind
To cry; I shut my marble eyes
Too afraid to scare a bird.

III. Wants to Know

Who is my father?
Why am I alone?

What must this field
Feel for the plow?

What does the crow love
Other than himself?

IV. On Graduate School

Grass for acres and trees tall,
Then, everywhere there should be
Some harvest to guard, sprouts
A building in which I am mistaken
For a broom, handled as such,
And given to the floor. To dust.
I am here to learn: that which fears me
Must be crow
In this hall of heavy doors
Where my body is a blemish.

V. In the Pulpit

I am a mouthless man of straw.
Fields of wheat wave around me.

Oh, my God, there is so much to sing.

I'm not dumb, but I wish I were.
A fool bothers the Father about a brain.

Hear us, Lord. There is too much to pray.

I am a mouthless man made of straw.
I hang to keep the crows away.

The fruits they pick. The murders they make.

When your Savior asked for water
They gave him vinegar instead.

Sweet Jesus, how long before you come?

I am a mouthless man of straw.
I hang to keep your children fed.

The fruits they pick. The murders they make.
Forgive us, Father, the use of our hands.

Again

You are not as tired of the poem
As I am of the memory.
A returning toothache
On either side of the mouth.
An ingrown hair beneath the chin.
Simple itch. Bruising scratch
And again I am bundled
In cousin Kenny's clothes
From last school year
My hand held by my mother's.
We walk as if the house behind us
Isn't warm enough
For my feet. In the dark
We make a few blocks
Around the one-story neighborhood
That I loved
Though nothing I've written
Tells you this.
I want to cut it out of me.
Because. Turns out it never mattered.
Right now my mother's asleep
On my father's chest.
His arm has landed
In the same place around her
Most of thirty years.
Give a man a minute.
She's asleep and I'm typing it
All over again. Everywhere
A man is shifting a bit
To make his woman comfortable
In his arms.
I should have told you this
Lines ago. We walked back

To the house we ran from.
Because.
My mother loves her husband
And his hands
Even if laid heavy against her.
I know you
Don't want to believe that
But give a man a minute.
We're not done.
My father loves his wife
And the shape of her body
Even if hunched in retreat,
Their son keeping up. I'm so sick of it—
Another awful father
Scarring this page too—
A bruising scratch.
We walked back
Through an open door.
And why don't I mention
He kissed my forehead
Before covering me
On the couch that was my bed?
Listen
And you can hear them
In the next room
Planning names for the youngest of us
Then making love loud enough
For the oldest to learn.

Autobiography

Keep the line steady   keep your back straight
Keep coming
Back for more   keep fucking
With me Cletus
Keep putting your hands on me like that
And you'll always have a place to lay your head
Keep my waistline down   keep your figure up
Keep your man happy   keep a woman crazy
Keep your daddy off your mama
Or next time I'm calling the police
Keep these nappy-headed children
Off my green green grass
Keep talking smart if you want to
Keep looking at my man
And I'll cut you a new eyelid
Keep looking me in my face
When you tell your next lie
Keep on walking I ain't talking to you anymore
Keep holding that last note   keep singing while
I get the splinter out
Keep singing for Jesus baby and everything
Will be alright   keep me in your prayers
Keep us in your thoughts   keep your eyes on the black one
He ain't got no sense   keep
Your money in your pocket Nelson
These hos
Giving it away   keep this one
Occupied   I'll get his wallet
Keep on living honey and you'll
Get old too

Detailing the Nape

It's our first summer at Grandmother's, and after our showers, she inspects the dark condition of my sister's neck, declaring it filthy. *You're not cleaning right. We've got to get that dirt off you.*

I peek through a cracked bathroom door as she and my sister wait over the tub until running water grows hot enough to kill bacteria. My sister kneels under the rush, a sinner prepared for baptism, while Grandmother scrubs as religiously as she scours the toilet each Saturday.

Grandmother takes a break to wring and squeeze the towel free of water, soap, and a bricklike, muddy dirt. *Child, all that noise isn't necessary. If you could see this nastiness, you'd be thanking me.*

Seeing my sister's distress, I open the door wide. *M'dea', I think that's blood.*

Grandmother quiets and bandages my sister well. *I'm sorry, baby, I didn't know you were that black.*

Track 5: Summertime

—as performed by Janis Joplin

God's got his eye on me, but I ain't a sparrow.
I'm more like a lawn mower . . . no, a chainsaw,
Anything that might mangle each manicured lawn
In Port Arthur, a place I wouldn't return to
If the mayor offered me every ounce of oil
My daddy cans at the refinery. My voice, I mean,
Ain't sweet. Nothing nice about it. It won't fly
Even with Jesus watching. I don't believe in Jesus.
The Baxter boys climbed a tree just to throw
Persimmons at me. The good and perfect gifts
From above hit like lightning, leave bruises.
So I lied—I believe, but I don't think God
Likes me. The girls in the locker room slapped
Dirty pads across my face. They called me
Bitch, but I never bit back. I ain't a dog.
Chainsaw, I say. My voice hacks at you. I bet
I tear my throat. I try so hard to sound jagged.
I get high and say one thing so many times
Like Willie Baker who worked across the street—
I saw some kids whip him with a belt while he
Repeated, *Please*. School out, summertime
And the living lashed, Mama said I should be
Thankful, that the town's worse to coloreds
Than they are to me, that I'd grow out of my acne.
God must love Willie Baker—all that leather and still
A *please* that sounds like music. See.
I wouldn't know a sparrow from a mockingbird.
The band plays. I just belt out, *Please*. This tune
Ain't half the blues. I should be thankful.
I get high and moan like a lawn mower
So nobody notices I'm such an ugly girl.
I'm such an ugly girl. I try to sing like a man
Boys call, *boy*. I turn my face to God. I pray. I wish
I could pour oil on everything green in Port Arthur.

19

Beneath Me

They were of a different hue.
They were all the same color.
The roaches at 51 Felton Street
Went to work when we snored.
They raced for black lines
At the flick of a switch.
They were an athletic sort.
Some of their youngest laughed
At my Chuck Taylor's,
And I just knew
I'd never make it to the Olympics.
Sleep and they'd creep
Into my ears come night.
They conspired with certain spiders
Regarding ladder and crane designs.
Anything to top the refrigerator,
For the loaf of white bread.
They did not fly
Because they chose not to.
They would not sing
Above a roach whisper.
The roaches on Felton ruled
The cabinets, the land
Of pots and plates and pans.
They were well-dressed and polite.
We sneezed. They said
Bless you. They coughed.
We slapped their shiny backs.
But I don't have to miss them
Coursing through the walls
I come from. All that crawls
Beneath me dies
When I try my walk away.
Every time I tell a lie, I smile

And imagine their coupling, oh
God, their loveless orgies.
Insects. Incest. 674 families
Below my family's beds.
The roaches at 51 Felton Street,
They hate my human face.
They know my last name.

Herman Finley Is Dead

1947-2005

The birds know a day
Made for defeat.
Not one of them sings.
Instead, they make a toilet
Of your newly-washed car.
Don't cry over it. Listen
To the birds—you, too,
Should shut up. But first,
Tell every alto you know
To hold her muddy breath.
Bid every obese soprano
A forty-day fast.
Get any man who ever sang
In a choir, head bowed,
None praying. Summon
Both the interpreter
And the speaker of tongues.
Pinch their burning lips.
Contact the necessary
Limp-wristed whose every suit
Is an Easter suit, bright
And loud enough to flame
In hell. I want them all
Wearing their worst black.
Call Nelson Demery
And Shanetta Brown.
Tell them to turn off the radio
Whether the station plays
Gospel or blues. Tell them
Herman Finley is dead. Then,
Tell them what God loves,
The truth: the disease
Your mother's mouth won't mention

Got bored with nibbling away
At the insides of his body
And today decided
To swallow Herman Finley
Whole. Tell them they must
Chop and torch each piano
Before helping me bolt the doors
Of all the Baptist churches
From Shreveport to Monroe.
I don't want a single hum.
We will not worship
Save for silence. Watch
The birds shit in peace.
When the choir director's arms
Fall, the choir must not sing.

PAUSE

Pause

From bed to dresser drawer
And all while rolling latex down
He'd whistle, and I felt
Daily at first, a chore, a long walk
Without trees. If anyone,
I should have known—
I who hate for people to comment
That I must be happy
Just because they hear me hum.
I want to ask
If they ever heard of slavery,
The work song—the best music
Is made of subtraction,
The singer seeks an exit from the scarred body
And opens his mouth
Trying to get out.
Or at least, this is how I came to understand
Willie whistling his way into me.
What was my last name? Did he remember?
Had I said? We both wanted to be rid of desire,
How it made even the shower
A rigorous experience. It driving
My coughing Corolla across Highway 90
At the darkest time of morning. It opening
His deadbolted door.
Us splayed as if for punishment
At every corner of the carpet. Then
Pause for the condom,
Elastic ache against death
Heavy in his hand,
And something our fingernails couldn't reach
Itching out a song. He was not content.
He was not bored.

If I had known the location of my own runaway
Breath, I too would have found a blues.
Poor Willie, whistling around my last name,
Wrapping his gift in safety. Poor me, thinking
If the man moves inside me
I must be empty, if I hide
Inside the man I must be cold.

Robert

A shame.
   I couldn't place the joy
Turning a white boy
   Red. Somewhere deep
Inside him I'd hear,
   Belly of the whale.
I worried about bruises,
   My brown burning the red
Permanent, how I'd look
   Left on a Bob, betrayals
Doubling. What if
   I hurt myself? God,
Dam the entire ocean.
   No one can hear a drum
Beat from the belly of a whale.

Open

I often lie open as a field. Sharecroppers have no fixed names.

Derrick Anything But

Derrick at the piano.
    Derrick under my car. Derrick stuck
At the bottom of a soup can.
    Look how his fingers go.
Derrick millionaire, stunt king.
    Derrick's in the cooler
Behind the last longneck. Derrick,
    Don't be so cold. I only sang
In the choir, thought
    I could keep everything awful
Out my mouth
    If I held the high notes,
But I swear to you, Derrick of the gorgeous
    Gold teeth, I further felt the spirit
Of without, absence
    Condemned to each hand,
Each time I clapped for Jesus. I envy
    How well you ignore an inner thigh
Itch, scratching at eyelids
    To claw back a stare. See
His fingers say no. How do you do it,
    Derrick up a tree? How hard,
How hot is the metal
    Under the neighbors' hoods?
How slippery the engines' grease?
    Derrick sweaty hands. Derrick baby grand,
Tell me the stroke of ivory as I sing.

Crickets

Again and in the proper key, we are
The sound of a man's back and the distance

That waits

And widens as he runs over us
Away from you, your screened porch,

And the glass of wine he dropped there,

Now a patch of splinters at your bare feet.
You could hurt yourself. Be still

And listen.

There is no such thing as background music.
All day we've wanted this kind of attention,

But you were humming

A love song—then hoping to hear him
Sing the lyrics. We wouldn't dare let you

Out of the night without us. Above us

You couldn't even hear glass
Shatter, what you thought he held, broken.

Grip

If it had become a competition in which we,
Like children desperate for the blue ribbon,
Pulled knotted hemp, gripping until certain
Of calluses, if our contest awarded the strongest,

The boy who could best inflict pain yet not
Flinch when injured, then you won, for I must
Imagine the brown of your back to reach my
Peak, a short thread of breaths, a tug of war

With the heaviest child grunting at the end
Of the rope until jerked and dragged over
The line. That fat kid flounders through muck

The way I splash your relentless name
In shivers about me. Watch him wallow.
If he tastes mud as bitter as this poem

Of mine, then I win—and you love me.

Fall

No, I do not recall the jump
Nor the reasons why. The dream begins with
   The plummet. Air tears
   At my skin. I crash
      Into the sidewalk, crack
      The concrete and my body (a fault line
      From shoulder to hip).

And now I am one of the crowd,
Circling the carcass with suitable murmurs.
I want to answer their questions,
Tell them the dead man's name,
But I cannot identify the broken body.
Even I don't know who he is.

Morning

A shine over the sidewalk. Like a woman's
Lip gloss. An accent. For the rooftops.
For the grass. Rain fell last night.

I missed it. Slept through every drop,
Fetal in a twin bed. So I wake
Certain that, upset with the weight of me,

The entire planet must have cried
Upward—tears beneath a man
Always a silent thing. Each cloud

Relents to light like the men in New Orleans
Who would say goodbye before leaving.
Would even mutter a concern. Was I all right?

As if their gold teeth might have blinded me.
As if they hadn't already numbed a pain.
Some late-night passerby has left

A cracker on the walkway closest to my window.
He probably dropped it, nibbling steadily until
The taste overtook his hands.

So much crumbles while we sleep.
So much soaks through. Think
Of what can happen when we doze

Like men dead in their graves—
The rain. A few crumbs.
A swarm of ants beyond the door.

Tin Man

In my chest

Drop a penny.

Cities shine gray.

No green is god.

And every tree must fall,

A missing beat.

Man made me.

Pull the lever:

So I stop.

Your whole world

The color gray.

Can I get you

Tired of your body?

Beat time:

a slit of air.

I can't feel a thing.

Never believe

I've watched color die.

slicing the air.

Skip it—

Add a little oil,

I chop.

I am tired

unpaved, green.

Don't you want

an axe handle

Use mine.

I won't feel

Don't say love.

Remember

the color green.

I've killed it.

In my chest

Hush, love.

drop one penny,

Men made me

of your woods,

Cities shine

something heartless?

for destruction?

Manhandle,

one damn thing.

Sean

A man I tried to love
    Handed me binoculars and
Explained the shrike
    Impales its victims on barbed wire
And rusty nails. Tiny but graceless,
    It knows what the world calls
Sharp, the quality of a point
    Perfect for piercing, for breaking
A small mammal's spine. I gave
    The binoculars back; I could not watch
The fowl at feast though I'd spend
    The morning in the mirror, wing and claw,
Then claw and beak until Sean
    Is no longer. I could sing like a butcher
Bird. I should clean my plate.

Lunch

In a fast-food line,
One man pulls a penny
   From another man's hand,

Grins too wide a grin,
And pays the extra change.
   The boy standing behind

The register takes my jealous
Stare for one of disapproval
   And shakes his head at me

To say, *I hate faggots*
Too. Carefully shifting
   My weight onto one

Skinny leg, I open
My appropriate mouth
   To order.

Idea for an Album: *Vandross, the Duets*

Turn the volume down.
Let me tell you something

About death. Men are
Like songs. I play them

While I can. They go
On about love, climax,

And end. I should know.
This is, after all, my body

Failing, like a song, to do
Anything more than touch,

And I am a man, risking,
As songs will, abstraction

In favor of voice. Take,
For instance, the voice

Of love, the man we call
Luther Vandross. He

Must have seen such love
Could not be unconditional,

And, like any man, wanted
To last forever, but I'll tell

You something about death.
For all we know, this music

Is as close as he came
To love before he died,

The way each man dies,
Alone. Turn the volume

Up. Show me one man
Who does not love

The songs he shared
With women.

Turning 26

You remember
Me pushing shoulder-first
Out of your body into
A spiral of birthdays
And bruises.
It must have hurt something awful
When I left you
To your husband
Like the mousetraps
He set so well. Now
I am full of cake. I am sick
With candles. I am twenty-six
And skinny
With a back too narrow
To bear a cross
Or carry a woman
From a burning house.
I ran empty-handed and can't reach
Far enough.
All because I hold a grudge,
A candle
Lodged at the portal of my throat.
But we should sing
Happy birthday to me
Anyway, at the same time
In different cities. Celebrate.
Light candles and make a wish
For me. I'll light mine
And burn like your house.

The Burning Bush

Lizard's shade turned torch, what thorns I bore
Nomadic shepherds clipped. Still,
I've stood, a soldier listening for the word,
Attack, a prophet praying any ember be spoken
Through me in this desert full of fugitives.
Now, I have a voice. Entered, I am lit.
Remember me for this sprouting fire,
For the lash of flaming tongues that lick
But do not swallow my leaves, my flimsy
Branches. No ash behind, I burn to bloom.
I am not consumed. I am not consumed.

I Have Just Picked Up a Man

A boy really,

And I am not fucking him.
I am driving

My car, not parking,
And I'm taking him

There, to the diner
On the other corner.

We will sit and trade names.
He won't tell his real one, but

I'll read to him.
He will shake his head

Or nod; he may not understand.
I have just picked up a man

And if he is afraid, he'll talk.
Or if he is hungry, he'll listen.

But either way, I'll read him
Some poems, glance at myself

In his eyes, and in the moments
Before I drop him anywhere

He wants to go,
Neither of us will be alone.

POWER

Lion

I wish you tamed. I wish what you fear—
A night alone in the forest.

A father who leaves you there. I wish you
Were ten years old again. And in love

With Marvin Gaye. I wish you saw his daddy
Shoot him. I wish you asthma. An attack

In the field. A lump in your chest. A doctor
Who won't touch it. I wish you'd live forever

Afraid of dying. See the circus and be content.
Animals crawling like infants for the men

Who made them. I wish you would
Sniff a man. I wish his whip

Sharper than fangs. I wish you could know
How bite-less I feel, the mouth

I don't close, his head in my throat.

Betty Jo Jackson

There's a story my father likes to tell.
    Never mind. My father's never been good
At stories, and I wouldn't want you calling me
    A gossip. Besides, this is about my mother.
I wouldn't want you calling her a fool. How
    Might you have handled things? You see
Your man approached by a girl whose hair is longer
    Than her skirt. Well, Mama was nicer
Than you. She simply moved from her place
    Behind the college cafeteria counter
And stared for a long time, first at the foreign
    Hands that held my daddy's elbow, then
Right into that poor girl's eyes.
    You know it—the look
A neighbor gives when, during a visit,
    You bump and break a perfect
Piece of crystal the shape of a dove.
    I guess you can tell why Daddy loves
This story so much, he, a one-eyed prize
    With a woman on each side of him.
To the left, a miniskirted Sapphire
    With red fingernails to match.
To the right, hair-netted, aproned,
    And ready to risk her work-study,
A woman you might mistake for Jemima
    If her eyes weren't fierce enough to push
A harlot away in whimpers. Betty Jo
    Jackson, I think, was the girl's name. Ask
My daddy. He won't forget: my mother
    Calm, but close to violence, she-wolf set
To claw and devour. I guess you can tell
    Why I'm so jealous of Betty Jo. She got
To see my mother back when she still
    Wanted a fight. I wish I had known Mama
Then. I would have loved her that way.

Rick

How I learn envy? I watch snow
 Cover the world whiter than you want
When you clean the tub. I watch
 The snow, gathered in a young man's hands and
Thrown across the yard to become
 The sting in another boy's face. Let's be that
Cold. When we die, Rick, let's leave the land
 Wet without us. Say you'll die
With me. Open your mouth. Say
 I knock on your door in the midst of a blizzard
Like those two Mormons you call
 A couple of Adams, *blond, clear-*
Faced. I'll be black with awful scars
 Below my eyes. Say you let me in. Say it
Like you mean it. I promise
 Not to proselytize. We can stand
In the kind of silence you frequently find
 In another boy's face. We can watch the snow
Make everything right. Just the way you
 Want it. Just the way I want to be. What
Would you do with me, Rick, if I were white?

Dark Side of the Planet

I have to believe in your body
Plant a tower upon your back

Turn the blue light and the red light
On and in separate directions

I have to open   think fault

In the earth   or whisper
You're the only one

Then split you in two
No   in half

Sweat and shed
Flex and pretend

I love
My own mass   its interruptions

I am sorry for my fingernails
I have to sing against them

Imagine one thousand
Cicadas

Imagine them   watching

Utter   your broad back

The backyard
Before the swing set

The sudden sun climbing
Toward us from the dark

Side of the planet
I'll have to lie

Give in to my mouth
Tongue and not bite

Worship your falling
Body if ever I am to lose mine

Shed and stutter   loose
The body   lose the race

You can't breathe a thing
I envy you your lack   of air

I have to take most the night

David

How best to hurt you.
  Fling a pitcher of sweet tea.
Leave
  All the lights on.
Phone your mother
  And threaten cremation.
Set fire to your cassettes.
  Call Hyman's dead moan
Effigy. Reply
  Singing, She died again.
How to kiss the first tear.
  How the hell you say,
But I love you,
  Though I'd rather hear,
Fireplace. How to burn you
  Alive. How to keep my man
Warm.

Your Body Made Heavy with Gin

I can relax. I smell liquor on your breath.
Soon your arms will be too heavy to lift,
And I'll watch the weight of you
Shiver while you sleep. But first
I want to see that stagger—
Like a boy sent off to battle, shot,
Then sent back. I kept one once.
He'd never get a good doze. Only quake
And dream of hands aimed at his throat.
He'd cough and gag. I'd shake him awake.
He was as you are. He could have died
In my bed. He could have never stopped
Dreaming. He'd take me
For the enemy. We'd fight.
But you and I won't fight tonight.
I'll remember some limping lover and talk
All I want about war. Or maybe
I won't. Maybe I don't care
Who survives—I only need to watch your body
Made heavy with gin as I hold you up
From your fall at the threshold
Because I love you and I love you best
With liquor on your breath
When I can get a good look at you
Just the way I found you, reeking
And too drunk to go after the roaches
With the heel of your hand. And too drunk
To take me for one of the roaches.

The Gulf

—*Galveston Beach 2005*

Seaweed chokes the sand
We won't have children

My lover's arms around me
    Natural like the falling sun

    What once burned
Clings to my feet

Salt inches
    Closer, salt stains the sea

    Something brown about it
The blood of those

    Flung overboard
    The word *ancestors*

The word *ancestors* in another poem

    To say the Gulf of Mexico is the Dead Sea
Today the Gulf of Mexico is the Red Sea

Its waves a siren of song
    Beware the dark

    Sand, the skin of my father
Will my lover look in his face

And call me his baby
    Kiss my black back

Or cut me open with a switchblade
The red, the Gulf, the sea

A song our mothers sang
   Arms around us natural as

My falling soul

   One mother jumped
   One threw us in

Family Portrait

My breath is also released
As I shiver onto my boyfriend's back,
Then open my eyes to the faces
Of my children, faintly

Sketched in white swirls
On brown skin—the only place
He can carry them. Out of my body,
They look less like me

Than like my mother and father
Who will die when I do. Their mouths
Poised to blame, I wipe them away
Before they can speak.

My Parents Snoring

A hailstorm leaves
Dents in the trees,

And still
They sleep. Bent and

Pushed to the ground,
Branches brush

The grass, a sound
Like her throaty alto.

Branches beat windows,
A plea for escape

His nasal bass.
I know this tune by heart,

Have never known them
Apart

From exhaustion,
A drizzle trailing a sudden storm,

A dirge for callused hands
At rest:

May they never dream of scrubbing.

Runaway

Barefoot in the actual dark, I packed a paper bag
And found the way out of my lover's house.
I had only the glass coffee table as obstacle; I slipped
Around it without stump or stumble. I left
The door slightly open; no draft lives in Louisiana's summer.
And how could I not move so quickly and away
When twenty years earlier I learned this skill—
How to shake the night's hand in confidence,
How to trust that no star will talk? I deserved this,
My anniversary—I had run from the sound of my father's sleep,
From his heavy, resting hands. I first noticed then
The front yard's magnolia tree, understood its promise to shed
And cover, that tree's duty to that
Smell and knew too my duty to tear like a switch through
Air, to strike the street's edge in a pair of tattered shoes,
Unconnected, alone. I made it
To Fairfield Street before the headlights of Daddy's pickup
    caught me
In mid-blur. But I left my lover better: I knifed a tire before I went
So no light could find my back, no right hand could break from
Steering. One fist clenched
My brown bag as I sniffed for magnolia and made a deal with
    the dark.

Why I Cannot Leave You

You bring home the food. I'm your hungry man,
Captive damsel dragged by the hair from her favorite
Streetlight to the trap of your tower, hollow icebox,
No magnets with things-to-do. No rules. It wouldn't
Be fair—you bring home the food—you can't read
Or write. I pace, check the window for my hunter. You
Bring home food and toss it onto the card table.
My teeth barely miss my fingertips—I rip
Into the bag. You like to kiss me, my mouth
Packed with the fastest franchise you could find, animal
Blood at each lip. Say carnivore, and I kiss back. I eat
My meat rare. You bare your sharpest grin. Bum
I say I love, you're my place to stay. We're against the law.
No one keeps me big as you. Fatten me, sweet ogre.
Get me some meat. Bring home food. Feed.

Track 8: Song for You

Bread or lightning, his hand opens like the hand of God above me.
His neighbors next door turn up their stereo to drown our sounds.
They must get tired of him putting me out every ten days—
It's the missing money or it's the man he caught me kissing,

And it doesn't matter; I don't love him. But I do love this song,
Every version of it. I never knew Natalie Cole recorded one, high
And helpless as the clouds her son reached for while she watched
The boy drowning. Hit me with some Natalie Cole or some

Donny Hathaway in his heaven of screams before he crashed
Into concrete. Or all 20 Temptations. The arthritic and diabetic.
The cancerous and violent. I refuse to choose. Nothing hurts
Like old R&B. God bless the couple next door—they muffle

Our misery. They must sleep close on nights this cold, a woman
With her man's fat hands all to herself. I pray she never has a son.

Like Father

My father's embrace is tighter
Now that he knows
He is not the only man in my life.
He whispers, *Remember when*, and, *I love you*,
As he holds my hand hungry
For a discussion of Bible scriptures
Over breakfast. He pours cups of coffee
I can't stop
Spilling.

My father's embrace is firm and warm
Now that he knows. He begs forgiveness
For anything he may have done to make me
Turn to abomination
As he watches my eggs, scrambled
Soft. Yolk runs all over the plate.
A rubber band binds the morning paper.

My father's embrace tightens. Grits
Stiffen. I hug back
Like a little boy, gripping
To prove his handshake.
Daddy squeezes me close,
But I cannot feel his heartbeat
And he cannot hear mine—
There is too much flesh between us,
Two men in love.

Because My Name Is Jericho

You would not believe me if I told you
    I met a man called Joshua.

I am not a city nor a saint.
    He knew where my body had been.

I named each place. Then after a long silence
    He played a song for me on his trumpet.

There is a word

    You will not have me say. So my mouth plays
Now as it did then, open,

    The broken bell of a tossed horn—
Each eye, my entire body, struck

    Open, dry
As it was that night. And maybe you're

    Right. Something had to be taken
From me. I was too beautiful

    To be such a sinner. He must have hated me
For that. Maybe some of us are

    Better broken into—we mend
Easy as a ripped shirt or

    A damaged wall.
If ever asked about damage I will tell

What I tell myself. I am overwhelming.
He was overwhelmed.

See. I am just as much a man
As Joshua. I've got the silence to prove it.

STOP

Liner Notes

Billy Strayhorn (1915-1967) wrote "Lush Life" while still in his teens. For her comeback in the form of a jazz singing actress, hip hop artist Queen Latifah performed the song for her role in the 1998 movie *Living Out Loud*, which yielded a soundtrack album said to be responsible for the reappearance of the standard in the repertoire of many nightclub acts at the end of the 20th century. The poem is dedicated to the singer Mary Griffin. The opening act and alto background singer for Patti Labelle, Griffin performed regularly at The Bourbon Room in New Orleans before Hurricane Katrina and her subsequent move to Texas. When not on tour with LaBelle, she now headlines Saturday nights at Club Groove in Houston. Griffin is also known for singing "And I Am Telling You I'm Not Going" (Holliday) from *Dreamgirls* in full voice flat on her back at the close of each show.

The radio staple "Memory Lane" (Dozier/Riperton/Rudolph/St. Lewis) was released posthumously by Capitol Records from the 1979 album *Minnie*.

By the time of the riots that followed the 1968 assassination of Dr. Martin Luther King, Jr., "Reflections" (Holland/Dozier/Holland) had made it to #2 on the pop chart. It was the first single and album released under the new name for Motown's biggest act, Diana Ross and the Supremes. While the group remains one of the most internationally known, "the girls," as Ed Sullivan referred to them for introductions on his television variety show, were accused of not being "black enough" in the late sixties and scrutinized by African Americans for their showtune-like, Vegas-styled performances. In 1968 and 1969, in order to regain and retain their black audience, Motown's founder Berry Gordy had them release the pointedly moral recordings "Love Child" (Sawyer/Taylor/Wilson/Richards) and "I'm Livin' in Shame" (Sawyer/Cosby/Gordy/Wilson/Taylor), as well as four top ten hit duet albums with the Temptations, *Diana Ross and the Supremes Join the Temptations* and *Together* and the *TCB* and *On Broadway* soundtracks developed from two successful television specials in which the two groups starred.

The epigraph in "Scarecrow" is from Strand's poem "Keeping Things Whole."

Joplin recorded the Gershwin standard "Summertime" with Big Brother and the Holding Company for their 1968 chart-topping album *Cheap Thrills* (Columbia). She died of a heroin overdose in 1970 at the age of 27.

Aside from recordings with Beyoncé, Mariah Carey, Janet Jackson, Cheryl Lynn, and Dionne Warwick, *Vandross, the Duets* might include "Everybody Rejoice" with the cast from the movie *The Wiz* (1978) and with the group Luther (*Luther*: Cotillion Records, 1976), and "There's Nothing Better Than Love" with Gregory Hines. Both were written by Vandross. Because he was such a diva-lover, at the compilation's most expansive, it also may be useful to include some of the recordings on which his voice is quite prominent as a background vocalist, like "Jump to It," which he wrote for Aretha Franklin. After years of battling diabetes, hypertension, and extreme weight fluctuations, Vandross suffered a stroke in April of 2003 from which he never fully recovered until his death in July of 2005. He was 54 years old.

The Reverend Marvin Pentz Gay, Sr. shot and killed his son, Marvin Pentz Gay, Jr., on April Fool's Day of 1984. The younger Gay—Marvin Gaye mentioned in the poem "Lion"—was Motown's top male solo artist in the 1960s and, because of his recordings from the 1970s and early 1980s, is known as a pioneer for African American singers who write and produce their own music. During his life, Gaye dealt with immobilizing bouts of depression, drug addiction, and paranoia over supposed attempts on his life. He was killed a day before his 45th birthday.

The quote in "Rick" is from Barot's poem "Eight Elegies."

"Dark Side of the Planet" takes its title from Pink Floyd's *Dark Side of the Moon* (Harvest, 1973). The album is one of the first of its kind, experimenting with environmental sounds and the latest in studio technology to create a kind of sonic excitement to accompany its philosophical lyrics.

Phyllis Hyman, from the poem "David," committed suicide just before a concert at the Apollo Theater in 1995. Later that year, Philadelphia International Records released her final album, *I Refuse to be Lonely*.

Donny Hathaway (Atco/Atlantic Records, 1971), an album of cover songs, includes the Leon Russell standard "Song for You." In 1979, Hathaway jumped from the 15th floor of the Essex House Hotel in New York City. He was 33 years old and had been intermittently hospitalized towards the end of his life. The Temptations recorded the song for their 1975 album of the same title, and Cole included it on her 1999 album *Snowfall on the Sahara* (Elektra).

photo by Sean Hill

Jericho Brown worked as the speechwriter for the Mayor of New Orleans before receiving his PhD in Creative Writing and Literature from the University of Houston. He also holds an MFA from the University of New Orleans and a BA from Dillard University. The recipient of the Whiting Writers Award, the Bunting Fellowship from the Radcliffe Institute at Harvard University, and two travel fellowships to the Krakow Poetry Seminar in Poland, Brown teaches at the University of San Diego where he is the Director of the Cropper Center for Creative Writing. His poems have appeared in *The Iowa Review*, *jubilat*, *Oxford American*, *A Public Space*, and several other journals and anthologies. PLEASE, his first book, won the 2009 American Book Award.

New Issues Poetry

Cynthia Hogue, *Flux*

Joan Houlihan, *The Mending Worm*

Christine Hume, *Alaskaphrenia*

Mark Irwin, *Tall If*

Josie Kearns, *New Numbers*

Claudia Keelan, *Missing Her*

David Keplinger, *The Clearing; The Prayers of Others*

Maurice Kilwein Guevara, *Autobiography of So-and-So: Poems in Prose*

Ruth Ellen Kocher, *When the Moon Knows You're Wandering; One Girl Babylon*

Gerry LaFemina, *The Window Facing Winter*

Steve Langan, *Freezing*

Lance Larsen, *Erasable Walls*

David Dodd Lee, *Abrupt Rural; Downsides of Fish Culture*

Lisa Lewis, *Vivisect*

M.L. Liebler, *The Moon a Box*

Alexander Long, *Vigil*

Deanne Lundin, *The Ginseng Hunter's Notebook*

Barbara Maloutas, *In a Combination of Practices*

Joy Manesiotis, *They Sing to Her Bones*

Sarah Mangold, *Household Mechanics*

Malinda Markham, *Having Cut the Sparrow's Heart*

Justin Marks, *A Million in Prizes*

Gail Martin, *The Hourglass Heart*

David Marlatt, *A Hog Slaughtering Woman*

Louise Mathias, *Lark Apprentice*

Khaled Mattawa, *Tocqueville*

Gretchen Mattox, *Buddha Box; Goodnight Architecture*

Carrie McGath, *Small Murders*

Paula McLain, *Less of Her; Stumble, Gorgeous*

Lydia Melvin, *South of Here*

Sarah Messer, *Bandit Letters*

Wayne Miller, *Only the Senses Sleep*

Malena Mörling, *Ocean Avenue*

Julie Moulds, *The Woman with a Cubed Head*

Carsten René Nielsen, *The World Cut Out with Crooked Scissors*
Marsha de la O, *Black Hope*
C. Mikal Oness, *Water Becomes Bone*
Bradley Paul, *The Obvious*
Jennifer Perrine, *The Body Is No Machine*
Katie Peterson, *This One Tree*
Jon Pineda, *The Translator's Diary*
Donald Platt, *Dirt Angels*
Elizabeth Powell, *The Republic of Self*
Margaret Rabb, *Granite Dives*
Rebecca Reynolds, *Daughter of the Hangnail; The Bovine Two-Step*
Martha Rhodes, *Perfect Disappearance*
Beth Roberts, *Brief Moral History in Blue*
John Rybicki, *Traveling at High Speeds (expanded second edition)*
Mary Ann Samyn, *Inside the Yellow Dress; Purr*
Mary Ann Samyn, *Beauty Breaks In*
Ever Saskya, *The Porch is a Journey Different From the House*
Mark Scott, *Tactile Values*
Hugh Seidman, *Somebody Stand Up and Sing*
Heather Sellers, *The Boys I Borrow*
Martha Serpas, *Côte Blanche*
Diane Seuss-Brakeman, *It Blows You Hollow*
Elaine Sexton, *Sleuth; Causeway*
Patty Seyburn, *Hilarity*
Marc Sheehan, *Greatest Hits*
Heidi Lynn Staples, *Guess Can Gallop*
Phillip Sterling, *Mutual Shores*
Angela Sorby, *Distance Learning*
Matthew Thorburn, *Subject to Change*
Russell Thorburn, *Approximate Desire*
Rodney Torreson, *A Breathable Light*
Lee Upton, *Undid in the Land of Undone*
Robert VanderMolen, *Breath*
Martin Walls, *Small Human Detail in Care of National Trust*
Patricia Jabbeh Wesley, *Before the Palm Could Bloom:*
        Poems of Africa